JENNIFER LEE

Writer and Director
of Disney's *Frozen*

Rebecca Felix

**Checkerboard
Library**

An Imprint of Abdo Publishing
abdopublishing.com

ABDOPUBLISHING.COM

Printed in the United States of America, North Mankato, Minnesota

062016
092016

 THIS BOOK CONTAINS RECYCLED MATERIALS

Design: Christa Schneider, Mighty Media, Inc.
Production: Mighty Media, Inc.
Editor: Paige Polinsky
Cover Photograph: AP Images
Interior Photographs: Alamy, pp. 19, 23, 29; AP Images, p. 24; Getty Images, pp. 5, 11, 15, 21, 29; Shutterstock, pp. 7, 9, 21, 27, 28, 29; Wikimedia Commons, pp. 13, 17

Publishers Cataloging-in-Publication Data

Names: Felix, Rebecca, author.
Title: Jennifer Lee : writer and director of Disney's Frozen / by Rebecca Felix.
Description: Minneapolis, MN : Abdo Publishing, [2017] | Series: Movie makers |
    Includes index.
Identifiers: LCCN 2016934269 | ISBN 9781680781847 (lib. bdg.) |
    ISBN 9781680775693 (ebook)
Subjects: LCSH: Lee, Jennifer, 1971- --Juvenile literature. | Motion picture
    producers and directors--United States--Biography--Juvenile literature. Classification: DDC
791.4302/33/092 [B]--dc23
LC record available at /http://lccn.loc.gov/2016934269

CONTENTS

FILM QUEEN

A blonde queen blasts sharp, glittering icicles from her palms. While the wind swirls around her, she builds an ice castle on a snowy mountainside. As she creates her new home, the daring queen sings at the top of her lungs, celebrating her freedom.

This **scene** is from *Frozen*, the most successful **animated** film of all time. *Frozen* tells the story of a magical snow queen and her heroic sister. Screenwriter and **director** Jennifer Lee wrote the film's **screenplay**. She was also its codirector. This made Lee the first female director of a Walt Disney Animation Studios film!

Many other special victories followed *Frozen*'s release. The film won 78 awards. These included Walt Disney Studio's first-ever **Academy Award** for Best Animated Feature Film. *Frozen* also won a Golden Globe for Best Animated Feature Film.

Director Jennifer Lee attends the premiere of *Frozen* with her daughter, Agatha, producer Peter Del Vecho (*left*), and director Chris Buck (*right*).

Frozen became a worldwide sensation. It is the ninth highest-earning movie of all time. *Frozen* is also the most successful film by a female **director**. As a child, Lee dreamed about working for Walt Disney Studios. But she never could have imagined how successful her work would become.

CHAPTER 2

A DIFFERENT DREAMER

Jennifer Michelle Rebecchi was born in 1971 in Barrington, Rhode Island. She was the second child of Linda Lee and Saverio Rebecchi. Jennifer had a sister named Amy. Linda and Saverio divorced when the girls were young. Jennifer later took her mother's last name.

Linda raised her daughters in East Providence, Rhode Island. They did not have much money. Jennifer was often bullied over her stained clothes and messy hair. This caused her to doubt herself.

Jennifer used her imagination as an escape, creating stories in her head. She also found comfort in drawing, reading science-fiction books, and playing video games. Her love for mystical

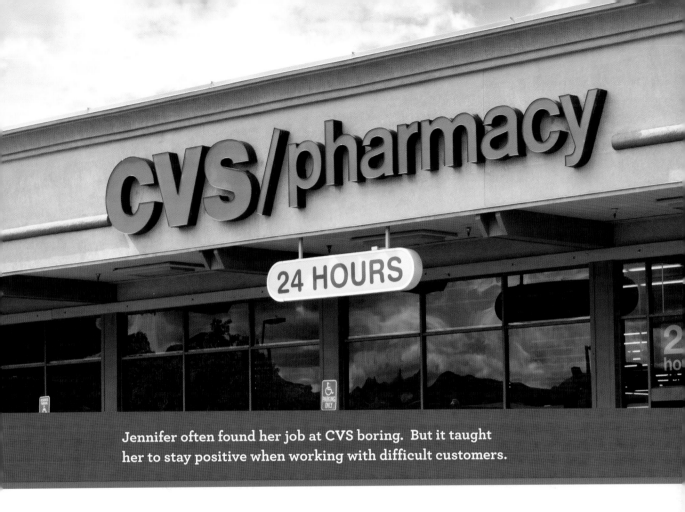

Jennifer often found her job at CVS boring. But it taught her to stay positive when working with difficult customers.

stories and cutting-edge **animation** led to her career goal. She wanted to be an animator for Walt Disney Studios.

At age 16, Jennifer got her first job. She worked at CVS Pharmacy. While it wasn't her dream job, the position taught her useful skills. And there was a more exciting career in her future.

CHAPTER 3

NEW YORK, NEW PATHS

LOVE AND LOSS

During Lee's junior year of college, her boyfriend, Jason MacConkey, died in a boating accident. Lee was heartbroken. But she was also motivated to pursue her filmmaking dreams. She felt that she owed it to MacConkey to live her life to the fullest.

Lee graduated from East Providence High School in 1988. She then studied English at the University of New Hampshire. In 1992, Lee graduated with a degree in English. She soon moved to New York City to work in book publishing. She got a job as a **graphic** artist for the publishing company Random House.

In 1999, Lee married Robert Monn. She also began considering a career change. Lee applied to

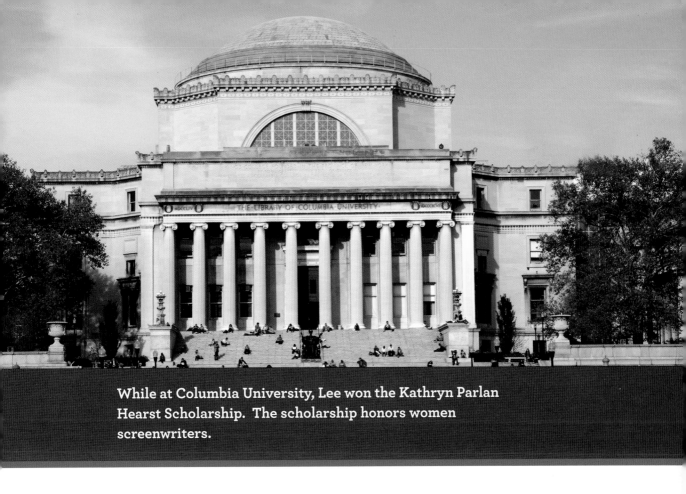

While at Columbia University, Lee won the Kathryn Parlan Hearst Scholarship. The scholarship honors women screenwriters.

Columbia University's film school in New York City. She began the program in 2001.

Lee felt different from other students. She was married and older than many of her peers. But on the first day, Lee met classmate Phil Johnston. He was married too, and closer to Lee's age. The two became friends and reviewed each other's work.

At Columbia, Lee began writing **screenplays**. She found she had a great talent for it. Her teachers and classmates noticed this talent too. In 2002, Columbia honored Lee with an award for excellence in screenwriting.

In August 2003, Lee's daughter, Agatha Lee Monn, was born. When Agatha was young, Lee and Monn divorced. In addition to parenting, Lee stayed very busy in film school. One especially successful project was writing the film *Hinged on Stars*. It won the top prize at the 2004 Columbia University Film Festival.

Lee graduated from Columbia in 2005. She had earned a Master of Fine Arts in film. In the years after graduating, Lee lived in New York City. There, she wrote **scripts** for small films.

In the spring of 2011, Lee's friend Johnston called. He had been asked to write *Wreck-It Ralph*. The **animated** Disney film would be about video-game characters. Johnston wanted Lee to help him. Lee's childhood dream was about to come true.

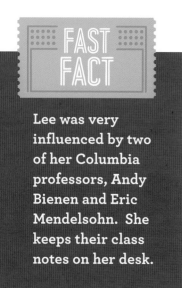

FAST FACT

Lee was very influenced by two of her Columbia professors, Andy Bienen and Eric Mendelsohn. She keeps their class notes on her desk.

Lee considered Phil Johnston (*right*) the most talented
person in Columbia's film program.

WRECK-IT RALPH

Lee prepared to go to Hollywood, California. She would spend eight weeks there helping Johnston write the *Wreck-It Ralph* **screenplay**. She brought Agatha with her.

Wreck-It Ralph was Lee and Johnston's first joint project. Since college, the pair had **critiqued** each other's work. But they had never **collaborated**. At first, Lee felt **intimidated** by Walt Disney Studios' famous and talented team. But she had no choice but to jump right in!

Lee described writing *Wreck-It Ralph* as filmmaking boot camp. Over eight intense weeks, Lee worked nonstop. She reviewed notes from story artists, wrote, rewrote, attended meetings, and more. Despite this hectic schedule, she fell in love with Walt Disney Studios.

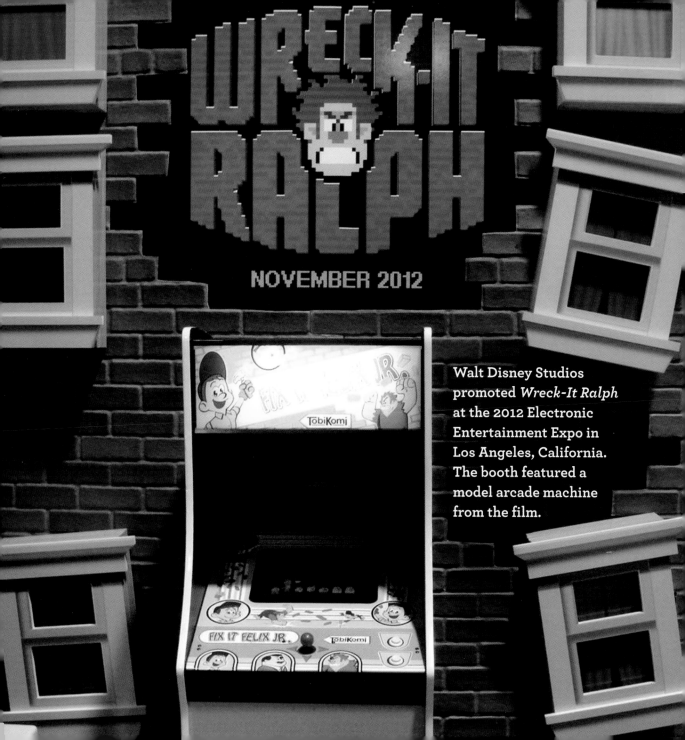

Walt Disney Studios promoted *Wreck-It Ralph* at the 2012 Electronic Entertainment Expo in Los Angeles, California. The booth featured a model arcade machine from the film.

Clark Spencer, a *Wreck-It Ralph* **producer**, appreciated Lee's hard work. He asked her to stay in California. Then she could continue working on the film until it **wrapped** in mid-2012. Lee agreed.

Lee's hard work paid off when *Wreck-It Ralph* was released in November 2012. The film was a huge success. It was nominated for Best **Animated** Feature Film at the 2013 **Academy Awards**. Johnston and Lee also won an award. They received the 2013 Annie Award for Best Writing in an Animated Feature Production.

Walt Disney Studio executives were delighted with Lee's contribution to *Wreck-It Ralph*. They offered her work on another animated film. But she wouldn't only be writing. She would be **directing** too!

Lee would be the first writer to become a director at any major animation studio. This was a huge accomplishment. And it was just the beginning of Lee's many record-breaking firsts.

SWEET STUDIES

The *Wreck-It Ralph* team visited candy factories, a bakery, and the World Confectionary Convention in Cologne, Germany. Their research helped make the movie's many treats look more realistic.

Lee attends Walt Disney Studios 2012 Animation
Celebration. She is joined by (*left to right*) actor John C.
Reilly, director Rich Moore, Phil Johnston, and producer
Clark Spencer.

15

MOVIE MAGIC

In 2012, Walt Disney Studios hired Lee to adapt a classic fairy tale into a movie. "The Snow Queen" was written by Hans Christian Andersen in 1844. The studio had been considering the story for more than 70 years. Lee would finally reimagine it as the film *Frozen*. She would **codirect** the film with Chris Buck.

Frozen's original **plot** was much different than the finished film. In the original story, Elsa, the character based on the Snow Queen, is a villain. Anna, the other main character, visits the magical Elsa for love advice. However, this story changed as Lee wrote the **screenplay**.

Most Disney movies focus on romantic relationships. Everyone at the company wanted *Frozen* to be a romantic love story. But Lee and Buck's team had a different idea. They wanted

The Snow Queen from Andersen's original fairy tale,
illustrated by Vilhelm Pedersen

Frozen to be about sisterly love. Lee began writing in this
direction, making Elsa and Anna sisters, and the final **plot**
took shape.

In Lee's final *Frozen* **script**, Elsa and Anna are royal sisters. Elsa has magical powers, but she is afraid to use them. She cannot control the snow and ice created by her hands. With these powers, Elsa accidentally creates unending winter in her kingdom. Ashamed, she exiles herself and abandons the doomed kingdom.

In most princess films, a prince would save the day. But the prince in *Frozen* is a villain. This was a first in any Disney **animated** film. The sisters are the film's heroines. It is their love for one another that breaks the kingdom's winter spell.

Frozen's **plot** twists made it stand out from Disney's other films. And the sisters' relationship was relatable for many viewers. Paired with catchy music and funny **supporting characters,** *Frozen* instantly took the world by storm.

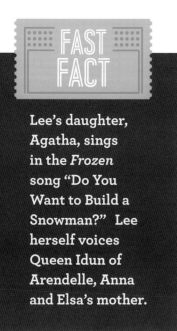

FAST FACT

Lee's daughter, Agatha, sings in the *Frozen* song "Do You Want to Build a Snowman?" Lee herself voices Queen Idun of Arendelle, Anna and Elsa's mother.

Elsa (*left*) and Anna (*right*) embrace. Elsa is the only animated Disney princess who is not a teenager. She is also the only Disney princess to ever be crowned queen in a film.

ON THE SET OF
FROZEN

Lee spent 17 months making *Frozen*. As **director**, she worked with songwriters, actors, and Walt Disney Studios executives. She helped select actors to voice the characters. She also worked with about 600 **animators**.

Lee and Buck wanted the movie to have a unique **Scandinavian** look. *Frozen*'s visual development team took a special trip to Norway. There, they researched Scandinavian clothing and **architecture** for the film. Animators also traveled to Jackson Hole, Wyoming, to study the way clothing moves through snow.

Lee reviewed and approved many sketches of characters and settings. She mapped out the

FAST FACT

Lee's office at Walt Disney Studios is covered in fake icicles. This is in honor of *Frozen*.

Live reindeer were brought into the *Frozen* studio. Animators studied the animals as they drew the film's reindeer!

Lee (*center*) celebrates *Frozen's* premiere with cast and crew members in Los Angeles, California.

entire film, **scene** by scene, with the **animators**. Some days, Lee reviewed notes and suggestions from as many as 150 people at once!

It was up to Lee and Buck to bring everything together to create a great story. And they did an excellent job. When *Frozen* was released in November 2013, fans and **critics** could not get enough. The film made a record-breaking $1.2 billion in ticket sales. *Frozen* was a hit!

LEADING CHANGE

By 2014, *Frozen* was one of the highest-earning **animated** films of all time. Even its music broke records. The song "Let It Go" was among the top ten most popular songs in the United States. It was the first song from an animated Disney film to make the top ten list in more than ten years. In addition to the **Academy Award** for Best Animated Feature Film, it also won for Original Song.

Critics praised *Frozen*, and the film won nearly 80 awards. Lee won nine awards for her work.

"LET IT GO"

Frozen's most popular song often gets stuck in viewers' heads. This happens to Lee too! But she doesn't mind. "I always say I think when I'm very old, the last thing left in my head will be 'Let It Go,' and that's just fine with me," she said.

Buck, Lee, and Del Vecho receive the Best Animated Feature Film Academy Award for *Frozen*. Lee is the first female director to have a film earn more than $1 billion.

23

Lee accepts the 2014 Dorothy Arzner Directors Award in Los Angeles, California. The award honors the importance of female directors.

For a first-time **director** to even be nominated is surprising. To win was an incredible feat!

That Lee is a woman makes her win even more special. Only 4 percent of Hollywood directors are women. *Frozen* helped bring attention to this unequal representation. The film's success was a huge achievement for female filmmakers everywhere.

Lee has also spoken about women directing more big-budget films. "The more women do bigger films as well, I think the more that will help. I think all we can do is keep pushing. And keep helping each other, just being very supportive of women in the industry." She advises young filmmakers to believe in themselves, and to let their **confidence** show.

CRITICS REACT

"The film represents a fusion of old and new both on-screen and behind it. Lee, who co-wrote *Wreck-It Ralph* (with Phil Johnston) and has sole credit for *Frozen*, is also the first female to sit in a Disney **animation directing** chair. She's done a **bang-up** job wearing both hats."

—Betsy Sharkey,
Los Angeles Times

"**I applaud the fact that the film gave us a sister relationship, rather than a romantic relationship, at the** forefront **of the story. But that does not excuse** *Frozen's* gaping plot **holes and the not-that-catchy songs (not counting 'Let It Go' of course).**"

—Caitlin Gallagher,
Bustle.com

The writers both reviewed *Frozen,* but their opinions are very different. Consider both sides. Who makes a better argument? Do you agree with one review more than the other? Why?

25

A COOL FUTURE

In March 2015, Lee's work caused another **frenzy**. That's when Lee's short film "Frozen Fever" was released. The short was just seven minutes long. But it created major buzz. Fans went wild for more *Frozen*, even before the short's release. Its **trailer** alone had more than 18 million views online!

That same month, Walt Disney Studios announced Lee and Buck would **direct** a *Frozen* **sequel**. This is a dream come true for *Frozen* fans. Meanwhile, Lee has been hired to adapt science-fiction novel *A Wrinkle in Time* into a film. The book is one of Lee's childhood favorites. Like in *Frozen*, the book's main character is a strong, smart female.

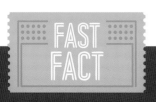

FAST FACT

To relax, Lee likes to watch TV shows on her computer in bed.

Lee and her daughter, Agatha, attend the 2014 Women in Film Crystal + Lucy Awards in Beverly Hills, California.

While Lee stays busy writing and **directing**, her daughter, Agatha, is her top focus. The two live in California's San Fernando Valley. Lee has accomplished her childhood dream of working for Disney. Along the way, she has won awards and broken **barriers** for female directors. But she's not done yet! As Lee put it, "I just want to keep telling stories."

TIMELINE

1971

Jennifer Michelle Rebecchi is born in Barrington, Rhode Island.

1988

Jennifer graduates from East Providence High School in Providence, Rhode Island.

1992

Lee graduates from the University of New Hampshire. She moves to New York City.

1999

Lee marries Robert Monn.

2001

Lee begins film school at Columbia University in New York City.

2002

Lee wins the William Goldman Award for excellence in screenwriting.

FAMOUS WORKS

Wreck-It Ralph
Released 2012

Wreck-It Ralph was released on the exact day 75 years after the first Disney Animation movie.

Won: Best Animated Feature Film, Annie Awards, 2013

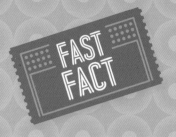

FAST FACT

The three things Lee says she cannot live without are her daughter, films, and music. Her favorite bands are U2 and Daft Punk.

2003
Lee gives birth to daughter Agatha in August.

2004
Lee's film *Hinged on Stars* wins the Columbia University Film Festival.

2011
Lee and Johnston begin writing *Wreck-It Ralph* for Disney Animation Studios.

2012
Lee is hired to write and direct *Frozen*.

2013
Lee wins an Annie Award for her work on *Wreck-It Ralph*.

2014
Lee's *Frozen* wins the Academy Award for Best Animated Feature Film.

Frozen
Released 2013

This film has been translated in 41 languages.

Won: Best Animated Feature Film, Golden Globes, 2014

"Frozen Fever"
Released 2015

This short film played in theatres before Disney's live-action film *Cinderella*.

GLOSSARY

Academy Award – one of several awards the Academy of Motion Picture Arts and Sciences gives to the best actors and filmmakers of the year.

animation – a process involving a series of projected drawings that appear to move due to slight changes in each drawing. An *animator* is a person who creates a work using this process.

applaud – to clap one's hands to show approval.

architecture – the art of planning and designing buildings.

bang-up – very good or excellent.

barrier – anything that makes communication or progress difficult.

collaborate – to work with another person or group in order to do something or reach a goal.

confectionary – sweets and chocolates.

confidence – the state or feeling of being certain.

critic – a professional who gives his or her opinion on art, literature, or performances.

critique – to review something, such as a performance.

direct – to supervise people in a play, movie, or television program. Someone who directs is a *director*.

forefront – the most important part or position.

frenzy – wildly excited or frantic about something.

gaping – wide open and very large.

graphic – of or relating to visual arts such as painting and photography.

WEBSITES

To learn more about Movie Makers, visit booklinks.abdopublishing.com. These links are routinely monitored and updated to provide the most current information available.

intimidated – to be made frightened.

plot – the main story of a novel, movie, play, or any work of fiction.

producer – someone who oversees staff and funding to put on a play or make a movie or TV show.

Scandinavian – of a region in northern Europe that includes Denmark, Norway, and Sweden.

scene – a part of a play, movie, or TV show that presents what is happening in one particular place and time.

screenplay – the written form of a story prepared for a movie. A person who writes screenplays is a *screenwriter*.

script – the written words and directions used to put on a play, movie, or television show.

sequel (SEE-kwuhl) – a book, movie, or other work that continues the story begun in a preceding one.

supporting character – a character that appears often in a story but is not the lead character.

trailer – a group of scenes that are used to advertise a movie.

wrap – to finish filming or recording.

INDEX